The Love Song of J. Alfred Prufrock was first published in *Poetry Magazine* in June 1915 and in *Prufrock and Other Observations* in 1917 by The Egoist, Ltd.

For my mother, who dared to disturb the universe.

ISBN: 978-1-63330-002-6

OBVIOUS STATE

Obvious State LLC
www.obviousstate.com

Manufactured in the United States of America.
Paper from sustainable sources, 10% recycled content.

Let Us Go Then

THE LOVE SONG OF J. ALFRED PRUFROCK
BY T.S. ELIOT

Illustrated by Evan Robertson

S'io credesse che mia risposta fosse
a persona che mai tornasse al mondo,
questa fiamma staria senza più scosse;
ma per ciò che giammai di questo fondo
non tornò vivo alcun, s'i' odo il vero,
senza tema d'infamia ti rispondo.

Let us go then, you and I,

When the evening is spread out
against the sky

Like a patient etherized
upon a table;

Let us go, through certain half-deserted streets,
The muttering retreats
Of restless nights in one-night cheap hotels
And sawdust restaurants with oyster-shells:
Streets that follow like a tedious argument
Of insidious intent
To lead you to an overwhelming question ...

Oh, do not ask, "What is it?"

Let us go and make our visit.

In the room

the
women
come
and go

Talking
of
Michelangelo.

The yellow fog that rubs its back upon the window-panes,
The yellow smoke that rubs its muzzle on the window-panes,
Licked its tongue into the corners of the evening,
Lingered upon the pools that stand in drains,
Let fall upon its back the soot that falls from chimneys,
Slipped by the terrace, made a sudden leap,
And seeing that it was a soft October night,
Curled once about the house, and fell asleep.

And indeed there will be time
For the yellow smoke that slides along the street
Rubbing its back upon the window-panes;

There
will be
time,

there
will be
time

To prepare a face

to meet
the
faces

that
you
meet;

There will be time to murder and create,
And time for all the works and days of hands
That lift and drop a question on your plate;

Time for you and time for me,
And time yet for a hundred indecisions,
And for a hundred visions and revisions,
Before the taking of a toast and tea.

In the
room the
women
come
and go

Talking
of
Michelangelo.

And indeed there will be time
To wonder, "Do I dare?" and, "Do I dare?"
Time to turn back and descend the stair,
With a bald spot in the middle of my hair—
(They will say: "How his hair is growing thin!")

My morning coat, my collar mounting firmly to the chin,
My necktie rich and modest, but asserted by a simple pin—
(They will say: "But how his arms and legs are thin!")

DO
I
DARE

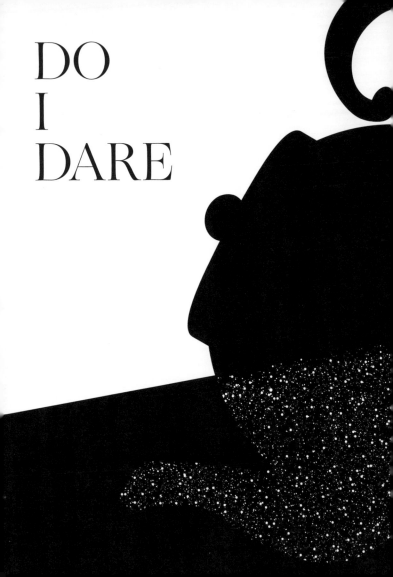

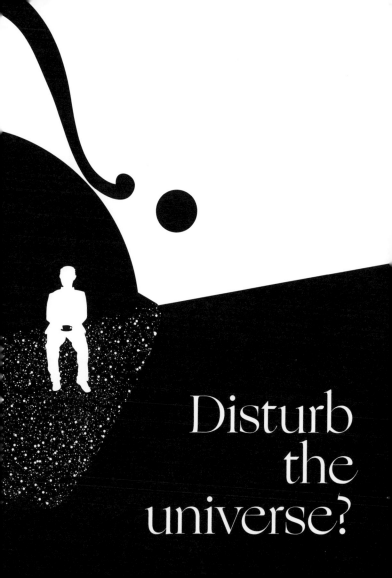

Disturb
the
universe?

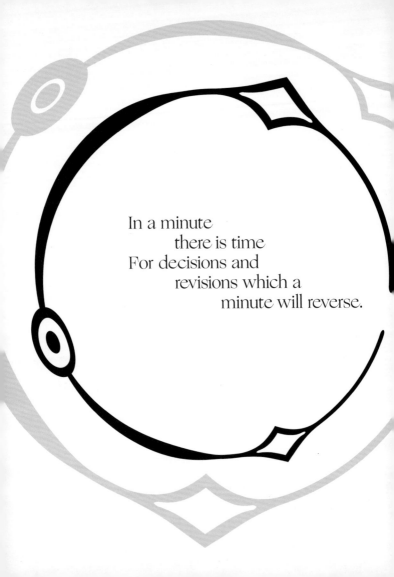

In a minute
    there is time
For decisions and
    revisions which a
        minute will reverse.

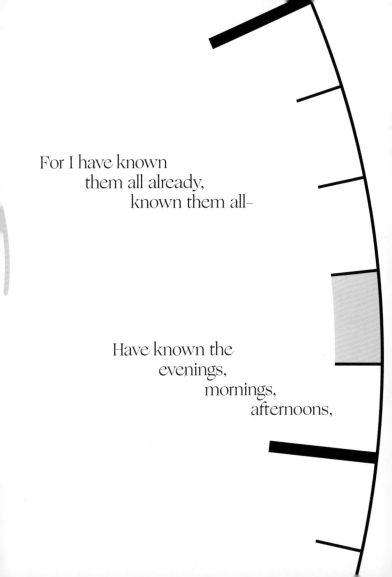

For I have known
them all already,
known them all-

Have known the
evenings,
mornings,
afternoons,

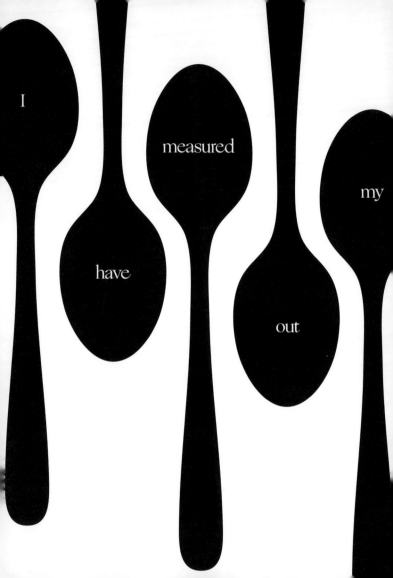

life with coffee spoons;

I know the
voices dying

with a dying fall

Beneath the music from a farther room.
      So how should I presume?

And I have known the eyes already, known them all—
The eyes that fix you in a formulated phrase,
And when I am formulated, sprawling on a pin,

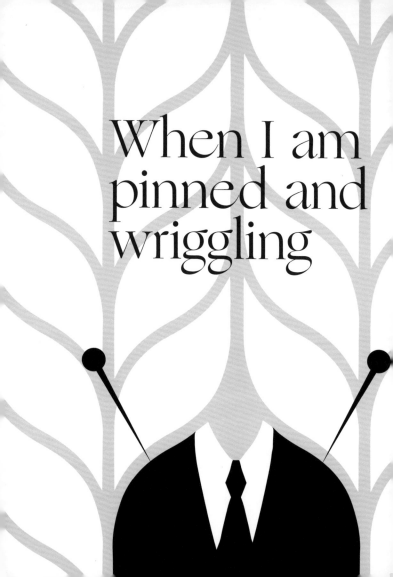

on the wall,

Then how should I begin
To spit out all the butt-ends of my days and ways?
And how should I presume?

And I have known the arms already, known them all—
Arms that are braceleted and white and bare
(But in the lamplight, downed with light brown hair!)

Is it perfume
from a dress

That makes me
so digress?

Arms that lie along a table, or wrap about a shawl.
　　　And should I then presume?
　　　And how should I begin?

Shall I say, I have gone at dusk through narrow streets
And watched the smoke that rises from the pipes
Of lonely men in shirt-sleeves, leaning out of windows? ...

I should have been
    a pair of ragged claws

Scuttling across
        the floors
            of silent seas.

And the afternoon, the evening,
sleeps so peacefully!
Smoothed by long fingers,

Asleep ... tired ... or it malingers,
Stretched on the floor,
      here beside you and me.

Should I, after tea
and cakes and ices,

Have the strength to force
the moment to its crisis?

But though I have wept and fasted, wept and prayed,
Though I have seen my head (grown slightly bald)
        brought in upon a platter,
I am no prophet— and here's no great matter;
I have seen the moment of my greatness flicker,

And I have seen
        the eternal Footman

hold my coat, and snicker,

And in short,

I was afraid.

And would it have been worth it, after all,
After the cups, the marmalade, the tea,
Among the porcelain,
          among some talk of you and me,
Would it have been worth while,
To have bitten off the matter with a smile,

To have
squeezed
the universe
into a ball

To roll it
towards some
overwhelming
question,

To say: "I am Lazarus, come from the dead,
Come back to tell you all, I shall tell you all"—
If one, settling a pillow by her head,
Should say:

"That is not
what I meant
That is not it
at all."

at all.

And would it have been worth it, after all,
Would it have been worth while,
After the sunsets and the dooryards
            and the sprinkled streets,
After the novels, after the teacups,
            after the skirts that trail along the floor—
And this, and so much more?—

It is impossible to say

JUST WHAT
I MEAN!

ut as if a magic lantern threw the nerves in patterns on a screen:

ould it have been worth while

one, settling a pillow or throwing off a shawl,

nd turning toward the window, should say:

  "That is not it at all,

   That is not what I meant, at all."

No! I am not Prince Hamlet, nor was meant to be;
	Am an attendant lord, one that will do
	To swell a progress, start a scene or two,
Advise the prince; no doubt, an easy tool,
	Deferential, glad to be of use,
Politic, cautious, and meticulous;
	Full of high sentence, but a bit obtuse;
At times, indeed, almost ridiculous—

Almost,

at
times,

the
Fool.

I grow old... I grow old...

I shall wear the
        bottoms of my trousers rolled.

Shall I part my hair behind? Do I dare to eat a peach?

I shall wear white flannel trousers, and walk upon the beach.

I have heard the mermaids singing, each to each.

I do not think that
they will sing to me.

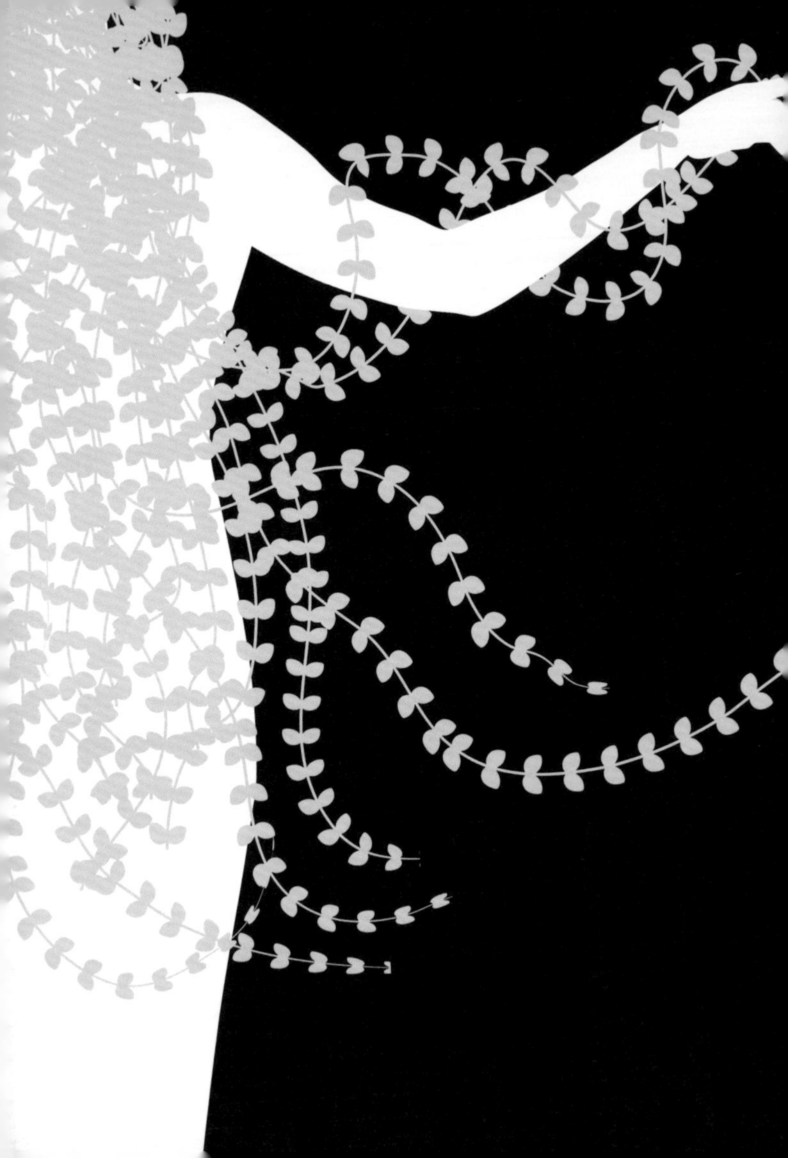

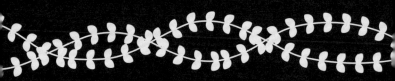

I have seen them riding seaward on the waves
Combing the white hair of the waves blown back
When the wind blows the water white and black.

We have lingered in the chambers of the sea
By sea-girls wreathed with seaweed red and brown

Till human voices wake us,

and we drown.

OBVIOUS STATE

Obvious State is a creative studio in pursuit
of wisdom and beauty.

We're inspired by provocative language
that has stood the test of time, poetry
that captures the beauty of the human
experience, and philosophy that drives us
to examine and re-examine.

We aim to create art and thoughtfully
designed gifts that prompt conversations
and bring aesthetic joy to everyday objects.

www.obviousstate.com
@obviousstate